USE THIS BOOK

In the Sunday School   It will add to the zest and interest

Young People's Meetings   Valuable topics are presented here, particularly in the doctrinal portion

Daily Vacation Bible School   These questions may be used, selecting those suitable for the ages taught

Pastor's Class   The doctrinal portion will help give the special training needed by young converts in the great truths of Christianity

Family Altar   These questions supply something different, yet they are in keeping with the necessary spirit of reverence

These questions will test your general knowledge of the Bible. Let us see whether you have read it carefully.

1,000
Bible Drill Questions

W. Burgess McCreary

WARNER PRESS Anderson, Indiana

1,000 BIBLE DRILL QUESTIONS

A PORTAL BOOK
Published by Jove Publications, Inc. for Warner Press, Inc.

Portal edition published June 1975
Fifth printing May 1985

Printed in the United States of America

PORTAL BOOKS are published by Warner Press, Inc.
1200 East Fifth Street, Anderson, Indiana 46011, U.S.A.

TABLE OF CONTENTS

HOW TO USE THIS BOOK

----

1. *In the Sunday School*—

There is very little time to teach the Bible when we consider the shortness of the Sunday-school period—just one hour a week. Too frequently the great fundamental doctrines of the Scriptures are not presented there. Call the intermediate or senior classes together during the week, or get them to come fifteen minutes earlier Sunday morning, and go through this book of questions with them.

The Superintendent might use these lessons in the general service of the school as a part of his desk work, thus insuring that his school gets these vital facts.

Teachers who are not well grounded in the fundamentals will find this course of study good as a preparatory course to the standard teacher-training course.

In social gatherings of the Sunday school the search questions, Bible spelling, and other parts of the book will add to the zest and interest. Just the thing for a spell-down or Bible games.

2. *Young People's Meetings*—

Where to get topics for young people's meetings is a great problem. Some valuable topics are presented here, particularly in the doctrinal portion of the book, which may be used either as the basis of talks, or for a lively question-and-answer drill.

3. *Daily Vacation Bible School*—

For the classes of Daily Vacation Bible School students these questions may be used, selecting those suitable for the ages taught.

4. *Pastor's Class*—

Young converts need special training in the great truths of Christianity. The doctrinal portion of this book will supply this need. A special class to meet just before prayer meeting or at some other convenient hour will prove of great benefit.

5. *Family Altar*

Frequently family worship is given up entirely because it grows monotonous and lacks in interest. These questions provide something different, and yet they are in keeping with the spirit of reverence that should characterize family worship.

1,000 BIBLE DRILL QUESTIONS

SEARCH QUESTIONS ON THE BIBLE

These questions will test your general knowledge of the Bible. Let us see whether you have read it carefully. They are especially good for a spelldown.

Old Testament

1. What high priest stopped a plague by swinging a censer between the dead and the living?
   Aaron (Num. 16:46-50).
2. What nation was saved by using moldy bread and old shoes?
   The Gibeonites (Josh. 9:11-27).
3. Upon what mountain did the ark finally rest?
   Ararat (Gen. 8:4).
4. How was the bunch of grapes brought from Canaan by the spies carried?
   On a staff between two of them (Num. 13:23).
5. What men were slain because they could not pronounce the letter "h"?
   The Ephraimites (Judg. 12:6).

6. What prophet who was neither among the living nor the dead did fifty men search for?
   Elijah (II Kings 2:16-18).

7. Who was the oldest man who ever lived, but who died before his father?
   Methuselah. His father Enoch was translated; so never died (Gen. 5:27, 24).

8. What great general was cured because he obeyed the advice of a little slave girl?
   Naaman (II Kings 5:1-4).

9. What king asked a witch to help him out of his troubles?
   Saul (I Sam. 28:7-8).

10. Who put his hand on the ark of God, and what happened to him?
    Uzza. He was slain by the Lord (I Chron. 13:9, 10).

11. What great leader did the Lord bury?
    Moses (Deut. 34:5, 6).

12. Who wrestled all night, without knowing whom he was wrestling with?
    Jacob (Gen. 32:24-29).

13. Who played he was a madman to escape from his enemies?
    David (I Sam. 21: 12-15).

14. What two cities were used to mark the north and south limits of Israel?
    Dan and Beersheba (I Sam. 3:20).

15. Who heard a voice coming out of a whirlwind?
    Job and his companions (Job 38:1).

16. Who was the first foreign missionary mentioned in the Bible?
    Jonah (Jonah 1:2; 3:3-10).

17. What man was put in a dungeon where he sank in the mud, for telling the truth?
    Jeremiah (Jeremiah 38).

18. What two men of Old Testament times fasted forty days and forty nights?
    Moses (Exod. 34:28) and Elijah (Kings 19:8).

19. Whose bones were carried forty years through a desert country?
Joseph's (Josh. 24:32).

New Testament

1. What man called himself a voice?
John the Baptist (Mark 1:2, 3).

2. When did a little boy give his lunch to feed a great many people?
At the feeding of the five thousand (John 6:9).

3. Who is called the "Beloved Physician?"
Luke (Col. 4:14).

4. Who was the first Christian martyr?
Stephen (Acts 7:59, 60).

5. What person did the Lord say chose the "good part"?
Mary, of Bethany (Luke 10:42).

6. Whom did Jesus say he would make "fishers of men"?
Peter and Andrew (Matt. 4:19).

7. Where is the shortest verse in the Bible, and what is it?
"Jesus wept" (John 11:35).

8. Whom did Jesus call a fox?
Herod (Luke 13:32).

9. Whom did Jesus ask for a drink of water?
A woman of Samaria (John 4:7).

10. What great catastrophe split the rocks?
The crucifixion (Matt. 27:51).

11. Who took the place of Judas among the apostles?
Matthias (Acts 1:26).

12. What magician was struck blind for opposing one of God's preachers?
Elymas (Acts 13:8-11).

13. In what city of Europe was the gospel first preached by Paul?
Philippi (Acts 16:12).

14. What man received a beating in a public place in Jerusalem?

Paul (Acts 21:27-32).

15. Who went to sleep in meeting and fell out of the window?

Eutychus (Acts 20:9).

16. What words of Jesus did Paul quote, that are not found in the Gospels?

"It is more blessed to give than to receive" (Acts 20:35).

17. Who was told to drink wine because he was afflicted?

Timothy (I Tim. 5:23).

18. When did a cyclone wreck a ship carrying grain?

When Paul was on the way to Rome (Acts 27:38, 41).

19. What governor's father was healed of a fever?

Publius' (Acts 28:7, 8).

20. To whom did the Lord promise he would give a white stone?

"To him that overcometh" (Rev. 2.17).

The Whole Bible

1. What prophet caused iron to swim?

Elisha (II Kings 6:6).

2. What baby was found in a basket by the riverside?

Moses (Exod. 2:3).

3. What three Bible heroes each killed a lion?

Samson (Judg. 14:5, 6), David (I Sam. 17:34, 35), Benaiah (I Chron. 11:22).

4. From what mountain was Moses permitted to see the promised land?

Mt. Nebo (Deut. 34:1).

5. From what mountain was the law given?

Mt. Sinai (Exod. 24:13-17).

6. What man led the children of Israel after Moses' death?

Joshua (Josh. 1:1, 2).

7. Whom did God say was a man after his own heart? David (Acts 13:22).

8. What was the first miracle Jesus performed? Changing the water into wine (John 2:1-11).

9. What Jewess became the wife of a great heathen king? Esther (Esther 2:16, 17).

10. Who was the first person to see Jesus after he arose from the dead?
   Mary Magdalene (Mark 16:9).

11. What prophet bound his hands and feet with Paul's girdle and then said that thus would Paul be bound?
   Agabus (Acts 21:10, 11).

12. Which apostle was banished to the isle of Patmos? John (Rev. 1:9).

13. Who was sold for twenty pieces of silver? Joseph (Gen. 37:28).

14. What two wicked sons of a high priest were destroyed by fire?
   Nadab and Abihu (Lev. 10:1, 2).

15. What apostle was bitten by a viper, yet suffered no hurt?
   Paul (Acts 28: 3, 5).

16. What woman was smitten with leprosy because she spoke against Moses?
   Miriam (Num. 12:10).

17. What wicked man was hanged on the gallows that he had made for another man to be hanged upon?
   Haman (Esther 7:10).

18. What general had his soldiers take empty pitchers to battle?
   Gideon (Judg. 7:15, 16).

19. What great king became like a beast? Nebuchadnezzar (Dan. 4:29-33).

20. What twelve-year-old girl was brought to life by Jesus? The daughter of Jairus (Luke 8:41, 42, 54, 55).

THE BIBLE AS A BOOK

Too little is known *of* the Bible, although much is known *about* it. Every boy and girl, and of course adult, should know the particulars of the Bible and its books, as brought out in these questions and answers. No Sunday-school teacher is properly equipped for his work unless he can answer them. Juniors should be drilled on the questions until they know them, and most likely the answers will stay with them through life.

1. What does the word "Bible" mean?
   The Book.
2. What are its two great divisions?
   Old and New Testaments.
3. How many books are there in the Old Testament?
   Thirty-nine.
4. How many books are there in the New Testament?
   Twenty-seven.
5. How many books are there in the entire Bible?
   Sixty-six.
6. Name the five divisions of the books of the Old Testament.
   Law, History, Poetry, Major Prophets, Minor Prophets.

14

7. How many books of the Law are there?
   Five.
8. Name them.
   Genesis, Exodus, Leviticus, Numbers, and Deuteronomy.
9. How many books of History?
   Twelve.
10. Name them.
    Joshua, Judges, Ruth, I Samuel, II Samuel, I Kings, II Kings, I Chronicles, II Chronicles, Ezra, Nehemiah, and Esther.
11. How many books of poetry?
    Five.
12. Name them.
    Job, Psalms, Proverbs, Ecclesiastes, and Song of Solomon.
13. How many books of the Major Prophets?
    Five.
14. Name them.
    Isaiah, Jeremiah, Lamentations, Ezekiel, and Daniel.
15. How many books of the Minor Prophets?
    Twelve.
16. Name them.
    Hosea, Joel, Amos, Obadiah, Jonah, Micah, Nahum, Habakkuk, Zephaniah, Haggai, Zechariah, and Malachi.
17. Into how many parts are the books of the New Testament divided?
    Five.
18. Name the divisions of the books of the New Testament.
    Biography, History, Pauline Epistles, General Epistles, Prophecy.
19. Name the books of Biography.
    Matthew, Mark, Luke, and John.
20. Name the book of History.
    Acts.

21. Name the Pauline Epistles.
    Romans, I Corinthians, II Corinthians, Galatians, Ephesians, Philippians, Colossians, I Thessalonians, II Thessalonians, I Timothy, II Timothy, Titus, Philemon. (Some say Hebrews.)

22. Name the General Epistles.
    James, I Peter, II Peter, I John, II John, III John, and Jude.

23. Name the book of Prophecy.
    Revelation.

24. Name all the books of the Old Testament.
    (See pages 14 and 15.)

25. Name all the books of the New Testament.
    (See pages 15 and 16.)

26. Who wrote the books of the Law?
    Moses.

27. Who wrote the books of History?
    Many scribes. It is thought that Ezra compiled them as we have them today.

28. Who wrote the Psalms?
    David wrote most of them. Some were written by others.

29. Name the writer of Proverbs.
    Solomon wrote most of them.

30. Who wrote Ecclesiastes and the Song of Solomon?
    Solomon.

31. What prophet wrote Lamentations?
    Jeremiah.

32. Name the author of the Book of Acts.
    Luke.

33. Who wrote the Book of Revelation?
    The apostle John.

34. In what language was the Old Testament written?
    Hebrew mostly.

35. What is the original language of the New Testament?
    Greek.

36. What are the first three Gospels called?
    The "Synoptic" Gospels.

37. What is another name for the Book of Revelation? The Apocalypse.
38. What writers of the Gospels were apostles? Matthew and John.
39. What writer of the New Testament was an apostle, but not one of the Twelve? Paul.
40. What writer of the New Testament was likely a Gentile? Luke.

BIBLE HISTORY

Most of the Bible is history. To know Bible history, therefore, is to have an intimate acquaintance with most of the facts of revelation.

The outline followed is not an arbitrary one, but the natural divisions of the Bible are taken into consideration. To learn the answers to these questions is to get a good general outline of the Bible in mind, along with some outstanding particulars that will help in a more detailed study of the Book of Books.

Old Testament

1. What are the two great divisions of Bible history?
   Old Testament and New Testament history.
2. Into how many periods is the history of the Old Testament divided?
   Thirteen.
3. What are the names and extent of these periods?
   (1) Probation; from Adam in the beginning of history to the flood, 2348 B.C.

(2) Dispersion; from the flood to the call of Abraham, 1921 B.C.

(3) Patriarchal; from the call of Abraham to the sojourn in Egypt, 1706 B.C.

(4) Egyptian Bondage; from the sojourn in Egypt to the Exodus from Egypt, 1491 B.C.

(5) Wanderings; from the Exodus to the death of Moses, 1451 B.C.

(6) Conquest; from the death of Moses to the death of Joshua, 1400 B.C.

(7) Judges; from the death of Joshua to the coronation of King Saul, 1095 B.C.

(8) United Kingdom; from the coronation of Saul to the revolt of the Ten Tribes, 975 B.C.

(9) Double Kingdom; from the revolt of the Ten Tribes to the exile of Israel, 722 B.C.

(10) Judah Alone; from the exile of Israel to the exile of Judah, 586 B.C.

(11) Exile; from the exile of Judah to the return under Zerubbabel, 536 B.C.

(12) Post-Exile; from the return under Zerubbabel to the close of the Old Testament, 400 B.C.

(13) Interval; from the close of the Old Testament to the birth of John the Baptist, 5 B.C.

4. Name a great person from each one of the Old Testament periods.

Adam; Noah; Abraham; Joseph; Moses; Joshua; Samuel; David; Elijah; Hezekiah; Daniel; Ezra; and Judas Maccabeus.

5. What was created on each one of the six creation days?

(1) light; (2) firmament; (3) land and herbs; (4) sun, moon, and stars; (5) fish and fowl; (6) land animals and man.

6. Who were the first man and woman?

Adam and Eve.

7. What are some other things mentioned in Genesis that came in the first period?

First child; sacrifice; murder; city; polygamy; music; metal worker.

8. Who were the three sons of Noah?
Shem, Ham, and Japheth.

9. Who was Israel?
Jacob.

10. Name the ten plagues of Egypt.
Blood; frogs; lice; flies; murrain; boils; hail; locusts; darkness; death of first-born.

11. What are the names of the twelve sons of Jacob?
Reuben, Simeon, Levi, Judah, Issachar, and Zebulun, (sons of Jacob and Leah). Joseph and Benjamin (sons of Jacob and Rachel). Dan and Naphtali (sons of Jacob and Bilhah). Gad and Asher (sons of Jacob and Zilpah).

12. What great city was captured by the Israelites at the beginning of the conquest of Canaan?
Jericho.

13. What judge was famous for his great physical strength?
Samson.

14. Who were the three kings of the United Kingdom, and how long did each reign?
Saul, David, Solomon. Each reigned forty years.

15. Who was the first king of Israel?
Jeroboam.

16. What king of Babylon carried Judah into captivity?
Nebuchadnezzar.

17. What prophets wrote during the period of the Exile?
Daniel and Ezekiel.

18. What book of the Bible tells something about the Jews who remained in exile after the return to Jerusalem?
Esther.

19. Who was the last prophet of the Old Testament?
Malachi.

20. What great world kingdoms ruled the Jews during the Interval period?
Persia, Greece and Rome.

New Testament

1. Into how many periods is the history of the New Testament divided?
   Twelve.
2. Name them and give their extent.
   (1) Birth and Infancy of Jesus; from the birth of John the Baptist, 5 B.C. to the flight into Egypt, 4 B.C.
   (2) Preparation; from the flight into Egypt to the temptation of Christ, A.D. 27.
   (3) First Year of Ministry; from the temptation of Christ to the Passover feast of March or April, A.D. 28.
   (4) Galilean Ministry; from the Passover feast of A.D. 28, to the Feast of Tabernacles of October, A.D. 29.
   (5) Perean Ministry; from the Feast of Tabernacles of A.D. 29, to the arrival at Bethany on Friday, March 31, A.D. 30.
   (6) Last Week; from the arrival at Bethany to Friday, April 7, A.D. 30.
   (7) Last Day; Friday, April 7, A.D. 30.
   (8) Forty Days; from Friday, April 7, A.D. to the ascension, May 18, A.D. 30.
   (9) Church in Jerusalem; from the ascension to Philip's revival in Samaria, A.D. 33.
   (10) Church in Transition; from Philip's Samaritan revival to the martyrdom of James, A.D. 35.
   (11) Paul's Missionary Journeys; from the martyrdom of James to Paul's arrest in Jerusalem, A.D. 57.
   (12) Later Apostolic History; from Paul's arrest in Jerusalem to John's revelation on Patmos, A.D. 95.
3. Where was Jesus born?
   Bethlehem, of Judea.
4. What is the only event told us concerning Jesus' boyhood?
   Visit to the Passover at twelve years of age.

5. What was Jesus' first miracle?
   Changing Water to wine at Cana, of Galilee.

6. Who were with him at this time?
   Mary, his mother; and his first disciples.

7. What great miracle did Jesus perform in Bethany?
   Raising Lazarus from the dead.

8. What are the names of the last three great parables told by Jesus, of which we have any record?
   Ten Virgins; Talents; Sheep and Goats.

9. What were the six mock trials of Jesus?
   Before Annas; before Caiaphas; before the Sanhedrin; before Pilate; before Herod; back before Pilate again.

10. How long was Jesus upon the cross?
    Six hours—from nine o'clock until three o'clock.

11. What are the ten recorded appearances of Jesus after the resurrection, before the ascension?
    To Mary; to the women; to Peter; to two disciples; to ten apostles in upper room; to ten apostles and Thomas; to seven apostles in Galilee; to five hundred children in Galilee; to James; at the ascension.

12. From what mountain did Jesus ascend?
    Mount Olivet.

13. Who were the first hypocrites mentioned in the early church?
    Ananias and Sapphira.

14. Who was the first Christian martyr?
    Stephen.

15. What Roman army captain received the Holy Spirit through Peter's preaching?
    Cornelius.

16. Who was the second martyr?
    James, brother of John.

17. Name Paul's most noted companions on his missionary tours.
    Barnabas, Mark, Silas, Timothy, and Luke.

18. How far west did Paul preach the gospel?
    To Rome, and probably to Spain.

19. Under what Roman emperor's reign was Paul convicted and martyred?

  Nero.

20. To what seven churches did John address the Book of Revelation?

  To Ephesus, Smyrna, Pergamos, Thyatira, Sardis, Philadelphia, and Laodicea.

BIBLE BIOGRAPHY

All that can be given here are just a few brief matters of interest connected with outstanding men and women of the Bible. It is hoped that these items of interest will stir up the curiosity of those who study them to know further particulars concerning them from the Scriptures.

Patriarchs

1. Who was the father of the Hebrew nation?
   Abraham.
2. What patriarch, when a boy, was put upon an altar to be sacrificed?
   Isaac.
3. Who was the father of the Arabs?
   Ishmael.
4. What great patriarch was sold as a slave into Egypt?
   Joseph.
5. Who was the youngest brother of Joseph?
   Benjamin.

6. Who among the sons of Jacob was an ancestor of Christ?
Judah.

7. Who was Joseph's father?
Jacob.

8. What was Jacob's occupation?
A shepherd.

Prophets

1. Whose prophecy is often called a "gospel"?
Isaiah's.

2. Who is called the "weeping" prophet?
Jeremiah.

3. What prophet tells of the "valley of dry bones"?
Ezekiel.

4. Which prophet tells about a great dream which a Babylonish king had?
Daniel.

5. What prophet was swallowed by a great fish?
Jonah.

6. Who among the prophets was a herdsman?
Amos.

7. Who prophesied that Christ should be born in Bethlehem, of Judea?
Micah.

8. What prophet was quoted by Peter at Pentecost?
Joel.

Christ

1. From what great Jewish king did Christ descend?
David.

2. Who was Christ's mother?
Mary.

3. How old was Christ when he began his ministry?
   Thirty.

4. What was his occupation before he became a minister?
   Carpenter.

5. Did Jesus have any brothers and sisters, and who were
   they?
   Yes. James and Joses and Simon and Judas were his
   brothers. We do not know his sisters' names.

6. How long was Jesus engaged in his ministry?
   About three and one-half years.

7. How old was Jesus when he was crucified?
   Thirty-three.

8. Was Jesus just a human being?
   No. He was both human and divine; both God and
   man at the same time.

Twelve Apostles

1. Name the twelve apostles.
   Peter, Andrew, James, and John;
     Philip, Bartholomew, Thomas, Matthew;
     James, the son of Alphaeus, Lebbaeus Thaddeus;
     Simon, the Canaanite, and Judas Iscariot.

2. Who was the only one among them except Judas the
   traitor who did not die a martyr?
   John.

3. Which one's name meant "rock"?
   Peter's.

4. Which two did Jesus call Sons of Thunder?
   James and John.

5. Which four were fishermen before they were called to
   preach?
   Peter, Andrew, James, and John.

6. Who was "the beloved disciple"?
   John.

7. Which one betrayed Jesus?
   Judas Iscariot.
8. Which one denied Jesus and later repented?
   Peter.

Paul

1. What was Paul called before he was converted?
   Saul.
2. Where was he born?
   Tarsus.
3. Was he an apostle?
   Yes, but not one of the twelve.
4. Where was he converted?
   On his way to Damascus to persecute the Christians.
5. How many great missionary journeys did Paul take?
   Three.
6. After the third journey, at what place was Paul arrested?
   Jerusalem.
7. In what city was he next a prisoner?
   Caesarea.
8. Where was Paul finally martyred for Christ?
   In or near Rome, according to tradition.

BIBLE GEOGRAPHY

Much light is shed on the Bible reader's or student's pathway if he knows where the events he is reading about took place. These geography lessons should readily be grasped by older juniors and intermediates who are learning geography in school.

A map of the Bible lands should be used in connection with these geographical drills, and each place pointed out as the question is answered.

Old Testament

1. Name five seas mentioned in the Old Testament.
   Red Sea; Mediterranean Sea; Dead Sea; Caspian Sea; and Persian Gulf.
2. What are five mountain ranges of the Old Testament world?
   Ararat; Caspian; Zagros; Lebanon; and Taurus.
3. Name five Old Testament rivers.
   Tigris; Euphrates; Jordan; Nile; Araxes.

4. What is the second largest river in the world, and how long is it?

The Nile; 4,000 miles.

5. What are the five lands mentioned in the Old Testament that lay near Canaan?

Armenia; Syria; Phoenicia; the Wilderness of Sinai; Egypt.

6. Name six great kingdoms of Old Testament times.

Egypt; Assyria; Babylonia; Medo-Persia; Greece; Rome.

7. What are the five important cities of Old Testament times?

Jerusalem; Babylon; Damascus; Hebron; Nineveh.

8. What is the most ancient locality of which we have any record?

Eden.

9. Where was the population of the world centered after the great deluge?

In the Euphrates Valley, at Babylon.

10. Where did the descendants of Japheth, the white races of the earth, settle?

Northwest over Europe and in parts of Asia.

11. Where did the descendants of Ham, the black races settle?

In the north of Africa, eastern Arabia, in the Mesopotamian Valley, and a strip along the Mediterranean west of Canaan.

12. Where did the descendants of Shem, the races from which came the Hebrews, settle?

North and east of the Red Sea, northeast of the Persian Gulf, and along the northeasterly shore of the Mediterranean.

13. What are five cities which Abraham visited in his journeys?

Haran; Shechem; Bethel; Beersheba; and Hebron.

14. At what five places did Isaac live during his lifetime?

Beerlahairoi; Gerar; Reboboth; Beersheba; and Hebron.

15. Name six places visited by Jacob during his lifetime.
    Lahairoi; Beersheba; Haran; Bethel; Hebron; and
    Egypt.

16. Where did Jacob die and where was he buried?
    Died in Egypt. Buried in Hebron.

17. Name five places in the Peninsula of Sinai at which the
    Israelites encamped in their march to Canaan.
    Succoth; Elim; Sinai; Taberah, and Kadesh-barnea.

18. Where was the land of Edom?
    South of Canaan and the Dead Sea.

19. Where was Moab?
    East of the Dead Sea.

20. Where was Canaan?
    In the western part of Asia, east of the Mediterranean
    Sea.

New Testament

1. What is the most famous sea of the New Testament
   world?
   Sea of Galilee.

2. Name ten of the principal cities of New Testament
   times.
   Jerusalem; Antioch; Ephesus; Philippi; Thessalonica;
   Corinth; Athens; Caesarea; Alexandria; and Rome.

3. How far was it from north to south of Palestine?
   150 miles.

4. About how large is the country of Palestine?
   About 12,000 square miles, or almost the same size as
   Massachusetts and Connecticut together.

5. Name five mountains of Palestine.
   Carmel; Hermon; Mount of Olives; Gilead; Zion.

6. What are five famous plains of Palestine?
   Esdraelon; Phoenicia; Sharon; Philistia; Jordan.

7. Name five rivers of Palestine.
   Jordan; Leontes; Kishon; Jabbok; and Arnon.

8. What are four brooks of Palestine?
   The Hieromax, Cherith, Kedron, and Besor.
9. What are the seasons in Palestine?
   Seedtime; October 15 to December 15.
   Winter; December 15 to February 15.
   Cold; February 15 to April 15.
   Harvest; April 15 to June 15.
   Heat; June 15 to August 15.
   Summer; August 15 to October 15. (See Gen. 8:22).
10. What are the principal occupations of Palestine?
    Farming; stock raising; fruitgrowing.
11. What city was the capital and principal city of Palestine?
    Jerusalem.
12. What great plain is the scene of many famous battles?
    Esdraelon.
13. What were the provinces of Palestine in Christ's time?
    Judea, Samaria, Galilee, Perea, and Decapolis.
14. In which of these provinces did Jesus spend most of his ministry?
    Galilee.
15. Name ten cities which Christ visited during his ministry.
    Jerusalem, Capernaum, Nazareth, Bethsaida, Sychar, Cana, Nazareth, Nain, Bethany, and Jericho.
16. In what territory did he spend the latter part of his ministry?
    Perea.
17. Name five cities in which the gospel had been preached before Paul's first missionary journey.
    Jerusalem, Samaria, Azotus, Damascus, and Antioch.
18. Name five cities Paul visited on his first missionary journey.
    Paphos, Antioch in Pisidia, Iconium, Lystra, and Derbe.
19. What country did Paul visit on his second journey?
    Asia Minor, and southeastern Europe.

20. In what city of Paul's third missionary journey did he stay three years?
    Ephesus.

BIBLE PLANTS AND ANIMALS

If a teacher uses a good Bible dictionary to get a more full description and explanation of the plants and animals mentioned in this section, these drill questions will be found very interesting as well as instructive.

Of course this brief list is merely suggestive. Other questions and answers on the Bible plants and animals could be made up by the teacher.

1. What kind of trees were used in building the temple of Solomon?

   Cedars of Lebanon.

2. For what flower was the plain of Sharon noted?

   The rose.

3. What vegetables of Egypt did the Children of Israel long for in the wilderness?

   Cucumbers, melons, leeks, onions, and garlics.

4. What city was noted for palm trees, and called "a city of palms"?

   Jericho.

5. What flower did the Lord say was clothed better than King Solomon.

   The lily.

6. What were "the husks" spoken of in the parable of the Prodigal Son?
   The fruit of the carob tree.
7. What kind of a tree did Jesus cause to wither, as an object lesson to the disciples?
   A fig tree.
8. With the seed of what tree did Jesus teach a lesson of faith?
   The mustard tree.
9. What tree did they use a great deal from which to get wood for the construction of the tabernacle?
   The shittah, or acacia tree.
.0. The likeness of what fruit was carved into the woodcarvings of Solomon's temple?
   The pomegranate.
11. What kind of birds once fed a prophet with bread and meat for a long while during a famine?
   Ravens.
12. What wild beast was killed barehanded by Sampson?
   A lion.
13. What kind of an animal once bit the apostle Paul?
   A viper—a poisonous snake.
14. What domestic animal ran in packs, half-wild, through the streets of the cities of Palestine?
   The dog.
15. What animal especially was a constant enemy of sheep?
   The wolf.
16. Name the animal that was used to carry merchandise across Palestine into Egypt.
   The camel.
17. What domestic animal common on farms today was it unlawful for Jews to eat?
   The hog.
18. What birds did Jesus say the heavenly Father feeds?
   Sparrows.
19. What animals did Jesus use to represent two classes of people at the last judgment?
   Sheep and goats.

20. What insect did Solomon use to teach lazy people?
    The ant.

BIBLE SPELLING

This section is especially valuable for a spelling match or "spelldown." Divide the company up into two classes, those misspelling words to leave the line. The winner, of course, is the person who stands up the longest.

Bible Men	Bible Women	Bible Countries	Bible Cities
Aaron	Anna	Assyria	Antioch
Bartholomew	Chloe	Babylon	Bethlehem
Cornelius	Damaris	Canaan	Cana
Demetrius	Deborah	Decapolis	Damascus
Elijah	Elizabeth	Edom	Ephraim
Festus	Esther	Galilee	Gath
Gamaliel	Hagar	Gilead	Gaza
Haman	Hannah	Havilah	Hebron
Isaiah	Jael	Idumaea	Jericho
Jehoiada	Jezebel	Illyricum	Jerusalem
Korah	Keturah	Judah	Kadesh-
Lamech	Leah	Lycaonia	barnea
Manasseh	Martha	Media	Lystra
Nebuchad-	Priscilla	Moab	Mizpah
nezzar	Rachel	Palestine	Nazareth
Obadiah	Rahab	Philistia	Paphos
Pharaoh	Rebecca	Phoenicia	Perga
Quartus	Rhoda	Phrygia	Rome
Rehoboam	Salome	Samaria	Sardis
Shalmaneser	Sarah	Syria	Shechem
Timothy	Susanna	Tarsus	Thyatira
Titus	Sapphira	Uz	Tyre
Tubal-Cain	Tabitha	Zin	Ur
Thomas	Tirzah	Zoar	Zidon
Uzza	Vashti		Ziklag
Zephaniah			Zion

OLD TESTAMENT INSTITUTIONS

This section has to do particularly with the tabernacle and temple of the Jews before Christ, and the furniture it contained, although the priesthood and feasts are also considered.

These Old Testament institutions were types or shadows of things revealed after Christ came, and their study is profitable from that standpoint.

1. Of what was the tabernacle typical?
   The church of the New Testament.
2. Into how many parts was Herod's temple divided?
   Six: Court of the Gentiles, Sacred Inclosure, Court of the Women, Court of Israel, Court of the Priests, and the Temple Proper.
3. Where was the brazen altar located?
   In the Court of the Priests, just outside the Temple Proper.
4. What did the brazen altar typify?
   Our justification through Christ's atonement.
5. Into what rooms was the Temple Proper divided?
   The Holy Place, and Holy of Holies.
6. What does the Holy Place, or first room, typify?
   The justified and regenerated state of a believer.

7. What furniture did the Holy Place, or first room, contain?

The golden candlestick, table of showbread, and altar of incense.

8. Where was the laver located?

Outside the Holy Place, near the altar.

9. What is the typical meaning of the laver?

Our regeneration through the Word of God.

10. What is the typical meaning of the Holy of Holies, in the inner, second room?

Our sanctification.

11. How many branches or lamps had the golden candlestick?

Seven, a number denoting perfection.

12. Of what is the golden candlestick a type?

The world-wide light of Christ.

13. What was the table of showbread?

A table covered with pure gold upon which the priests placed twelve loaves of bread each seventh day.

14. What does this showbread typify?

Christ, the bread of life, our spiritual food.

15. What did the offering of the incense upon the altar typify?

The offerings of the prayers of God's people.

16. What did the blood on the horns of this altar typify?

The entire sanctification of believers.

17. What furniture did the Holy of Holies contain?

The ark of the covenant and the mercy seat.

18. What did the ark and the mercy seat typify?

God's mercy and justice; the ark is the symbol of his violated law, and the mercy seat is the symbol of the atonement for the sin of its violation.

19. Of what three classes was the Israelitish priesthood composed?

The Levites; priests, and high priest.

20. Who was the first high priest?

Aaron.

21. Who became the high priest after him?
    The eldest son among his descendants.
22. The high priest was typical of whom?
    Christ.
23. Who were the common priests?
    The other sons of Aaron.
24. The common priests were typical of whom?
    God's people.
25. What are the two main classes of sacrifices offered under the law of Moses?
    Sweet-savor offerings and sin-offerings.
26. What were the five offerings made under the Old Testament dispensation?
    Burnt, meal- and peace-offerings; sin- and trespass-offerings.
27. Of what were these offerings types?
    The atonement of Christ, and the dedication of believers to him.
28. What were the three greatest sacred feasts of the Jews?
    Passover; Pentecost; Feast of Tabernacles.
29. Of what was the Passover typical?
    Of Christ, our passover.
30. Pentecost?
    Of the consecration of the Christian to God.
31. Tabernacles?
    Of praise and thanksgiving of the Christian for deliverance from sin.
32. What were the three lesser feasts?
    Trumpets, Dedication, and Purim.
33. On what day each year did the high priest enter the Holy of Holies?
    On the Day of Atonement.
34. During what feast of the Jews was Christ crucified?
    At the feast of the Passover.
35. What great event in the Christian church took place at Pentecost?
    The descent of the Holy Ghost.

36. What was the Feast of Purim in memory of?
    The deliverance of the Jews by Queen Esther from the
    massacre planned by Haman.
37. Of what is leprosy and its cleansing a type?
    Of sin, and our cleansing from it.
38. What does the Nazarite vow typify?
    An entire consecration to God.
39. What is the typical meaning of the Israelites' journey
    from Egypt to Canaan?
    The journey of the Christian from sin to holiness.
40. Of what is the Babylonish captivity typical?
    Of the bondage of God's people in harmful religious
    systems that divide them, and of their restoration to
    the unity the Lord prayed for.

HOW WE GOT OUR BIBLE

Where did our English or American Bible come from? This is important. It has a long history, and some things concerning that history should be known by everybody who reads the Bible. Such a knowledge will help confirm our faith in the Book and rid us of prejudice which might not be warranted, for any particular version.

1. What are the three best English translations of the Bible today?

   The Authorized, Revised, and American Standard Versions.

2. What was the original language of the Old Testament?

   Hebrew with a few sections in Aramaic.

3. What was the original language of the New Testament?

   Greek.

4. Are these languages as used in the Scripture spoken today?

   No. They are "dead" languages. Modern Greek differs from the Greek of the New Testament.

5. What is the oldest translation of the Old Testament we have?

   The Septuagint (LXX).

6. When, where, and into what language was it translated?

In the third century B.C., at Alexandria, Egypt, from Hebrew into Greek.

7. What Bible does the Roman Catholic Church use?
The Douay-Rheims Version.

8. From what was this version translated?
The Latin Vulgate, a great Latin translation made by Jerome about A.D. 400, approved by the Council of Trent in 1546.

9. Into what language was a translation of the Bible made in the second century A.D.?
Syriac, by Christians of northern Syria.

10. What versions were used by the early Christian church?
Septuagint, Latin Vulgate, and Syriac.

11. Who translated the first Bible into English?
Wycliffe (1380).

12. Who first translated the Bible into English free from the original languages?
Tyndale (1525-1530).

13. How did Tyndale meet his death?
He was strangled and burned at the stake through the influence of the Roman Catholic Church against him.

14. What were some other versions in common use in Tyndale's day?
Matthew Coverdale's, and the Great Bible.

15. During the reign of Queen Elizabeth (1558-1603) what Bibles were published?
The Geneva Version (1560); the Bishop's Bible (1568); and the Rheims New Testament (Roman Catholic, 1582).

16. During what English King's reign was the Authorized Version published?
James I (1603-25). It was produced in 1611.

17. Why is a revision of the Authorized Version valuable?

After 1611 many valuable manuscripts of the Bible, older and nearer the original than any before known were found. Too, the English language has changed a great deal.

18. What year was the Revised Version completed?
1885.

19. Who prepared this revision?
A British and American Revision Committee made up of leading British and American biblical scholars.

20. Who prepared the American Standard Version and when?
The American Revision Committee, in 1901.

STUDY OF BIBLE DOCTRINE

This section is a simplified treatment of the main themes of Christian theology. It contains the fundamentals of the faith which all evangelical Christians believe, and which should be known by ourselves and our children. Every Christian loves these precious doctrines, which are all made prominent in Holy Writ.

Drills in these questions and answers will be productive of great good in the home, Sunday school, or elsewhere.

Our Heavenly Father

1. What does the Bible take for granted concerning God?
   The existence of God.
2. How do we know there is a God?
   There must be a first cause of all things; judging from nature, the first cause is an intelligent person; and judging from the nature of man, his creation, he must be a moral governor. The God of the Bible is just such an intelligent, moral, personal First Cause.
3. What rightfully belongs to God?
   All things. He created all.

4. What great truth did Jesus tell us concerning God?
   That he is our Heavenly Father.

5. What is the nature of God's being?
   "God is a Spirit" (John 4:24).

6. Does he have a material body as we have?
   No. Jesus said, "A spirit hath not flesh and bones" (Luke 24:39).

7. How long has God lived?
   Always.

8. How long will he yet live?
   Always. "From everlasting to everlasting" (Ps. 90:2).

9. Where does God dwell?
   In heaven.

10. Where else does he dwell?
    On earth, with his people: "I dwell . . . with him also that is of a contrite and humble spirit" (Isa. 57:15).
    He is present everywhere.

11. How many gods are there?
    There is only one real God.

12. Is it right to worship anyone but God?
    No. To worship anything else is idol worship. "Little children, keep yourselves from idols" (I John 5:21).

13. Can we hide from God.
    No, for he is everywhere.

14. What does God think of sin?
    He hates sin.

15. What does God think of the wicked sinner who loves his sins?
    "God is angry with the wicked every day" (Ps. 7:11).

16. Does God love every one then?
    Yes, even though he is angry with the sinner He loves him and wants him to get saved.

17. How great is God's love?
    So great that He is called love—"God is love" (I John 4:8).

18. How has His love been shown to us?
    By giving Christ to the world.

19. Does God give us everything we want?
    No, He knows we ought not to have some things.
20. Does he give us what we need?
    Yes. He cares for us.
21. Can we see God?
    "No man hath seen God at any time" (I John 1:18).
22. Does God ever make a mistake?
    No. He is all-wise.
23. How does God show His mercy to us?
    In saving us and giving us life and health.
24. Are there some to whom God will not show mercy?
    Yes. "He shall have judgment without mercy, that hath
    showed no mercy" (Jas. 2:13).
25. How great is God's power?
    He is all-powerful.
26. How did he manifest his power after Jesus was put in
    the tomb?
    By resurrecting him.
27. How does he show his power in the world today?
    Through his church.
28. What are some of the ways in which God has shown
    his great power?
    In miracles: saving people, healing them, raising the
    dead, and casting out devils.
29. What does God's power help the Christians to do?
    To conquer sin and Satan.
30. Can we stay true to God without this power?
    No.
31. How do we get it?
    By asking for it—praying.
32. What will God's power help us to do with bad habits?
    Get rid of them.
33. Is God a person?
    Yes. Some day we shall see him (Matt. 5:8).
34. Is Christ a person?
    Yes, he is "gone into heaven and is on the right hand
    of God" (I Pet. 3:22).

35. Is the Holy Ghost a person?
   Yes. Jesus said, "He" would do many things when "He" came.

36. Are these three persons each God?
   No. There are three persons in God, but only one God. "These *three* are one" (I John 5:7).

37. What do we call these three persons who are one God? The Trinity.

38. Do they all have the same attributes?
   Yes. They are equal.

39. May we pray to either of these persons?
   Yes.

40. Can we understand all about the Trinity?
   Not until we get to heaven.

Christ, Our Savior

1. What relation is Christ to the heavenly Father?
   He is "the Son of the living God" (Matt. 16:15-17).

2. What other names are given to Christ?
   Messiah; Son of Man; Jesus; Savior.

3. What does Messiah mean?
   The "anointed" one, or the King who should come and deliver Israel.

4. What is the meaning of Son of Man?
   It means that Christ was human as well as divine.

5. Why was he called Jesus?
   It means "God is salvation," and it was given Jesus because "he shall save his people from their sins" (Matt. 1:21).

6. What does "Christ" mean?
   It is the Greek word for Messiah.

7. How do we know that Christ is God?
   Isaiah calls him "the mighty God" (Isa. 9:6).

8. Is it proper to pray to Jesus?
   Yes. Every knee should bow to him (Phil. 2:10).

9. Is Jesus still active in the world?
   Yes. He said, "Lo, I am with you always" (Matt. 28:20).

10. Why did he come to earth as the Son of Man?
    "To seek and to save that which was lost" (Luke 19:10).

11. How do we know that Christ was human as well as divine?
    He is called "the man Christ Jesus" (I Tim. 2:5).

12. Who was his father and mother?
    The virgin Mary was his mother, and God his father.

13. From what great patriarch did he descend?
    Abraham.

14. Yet, did he live before Abraham?
    Yes, for he said, "Before Abraham was, I am" (John 8:58).

15. What was the threefold aspect of Jesus' Messiahship?
    He was Prophet, Priest, and King.

16. Was Jesus' human growth and development much like any other boy's?
    Yes. He "increased [or developed] in wisdom [mentally] and stature [physically] and in favor with God [spiritually] and man [socially]."

17. Did Jesus have human appetites and weaknesses?
    Yes. He hungered, thirsted, became weary, wept, and died.

18. Why was he human as well as divine?
    Being man, he lifted us up to God, and being God, he brought God close to us.

19. Did Jesus have any temptations to sin?
    He "was in all points tempted like as we are, yet without sin" (Heb. 4:15).

20. What humble men visited the baby Jesus at his birth?
    Shepherds of Bethlehem.

21. What noted men visited him sometime later?
    Wise men from the east.

22. To what country did Joseph and Mary take Jesus to keep the baby Jesus from being killed?
Egypt.

23. How old was he when he talked with the doctors in the temple.
Twelve.

24. Who baptized Jesus?
John the Baptist.

25. How long did Jesus fast before his temptations in the wilderness?
Forty days and forty nights.

26. What is the greatest sermon of which we have any record?
The Sermon on the Mount.

27. What great Jewish ruler did Jesus talk with by night in Jerusalem?
Nicodemus.

28. With whom did Jesus speak on his way through Samaria, at Jacob's well?
A woman of Sychar.

29. What two great sects among the Jews were prominent in rejecting Jesus?
Pharisees and Sadducees.

30. What words uttered by Jesus on the cross showed his humanity?
"I thirst."

31. With what body did Jesus rise from the tomb?
With the same body that went into the tomb.

32. Did Jesus ever perform any miracles purely for his own benefit?
No. They were always for the benefit of others.

33. How did Jesus show he was lord of nature?
He walked on the waves, and stilled the wind.

34. How did he show he had power over disease?
He healed the sick.

35. How did he prove his power over death?
He raised the dead and came from the tomb himself.

36. Has he lost any of His power?
    No. "Jesus Christ the same yesterday, and today, and forever" (Heb. 13:8).

37. What commission did Christ give his followers?
    "Go ye therefore, and teach all nations, baptizing them in the name of the Father, and of the Son, and of the Holy Ghost" (Matt. 28:19).

38. Has Christ's last command been carried out yet?
    No. There is yet much territory to gain.

39. What great institution did Christ found when on earth that is carrying out this commission?
    His church.

40. What are Christ's followers called?
    Christians.

The Holy Spirit

1. Who is the Holy Spirit?
   One of the persons in the divine Trinity.

2. By what other name is he known?
   The Holy Ghost.

3. Is he eternal, like God and Christ?
   Yes. He is called the "eternal spirit" (Heb. 9:14).

4. Where in the Bible do we first read of him?
   In Gen. 1:2—"The Spirit of God moved upon the face of the waters."

5. Why was he sent to earth?
   To carry on Jesus' work in the earth.

6. What did he do to help in giving us the Holy Scriptures?
   He inspired the writers so that "they were moved by the Holy Ghost" (II Pet. 1:21).

7. When did he descend, and where is the event recorded?
   At Pentecost (See Acts 2).

8. Is he still here carrying on his work?
   Yes.

9. What does the Spirit do for the sinful world?
   He "reproves the world of sin," that is, he convicts sinners (see John 16:8).

10. What does this conviction cause sinners to do?
    It awakens them to turn to Christ.

11. When the sinner turns to God what does the Holy Spirit do for him?
    Converts him and guides him into the truth.

12. How does he work as Comforter?
    He comes to dwell in the pure of heart.

13. Can we grieve the Holy Spirit?
    Yes. "Grieve not the Holy Spirit of God" (Eph. 4:30).

14. Is it possible to sin against him?
    Yes.

15. What is a form of sin against the Holy Spirit?
    Turning his pleadings away until there is no more possibility of repentance.

16. Has a person sinned against the Spirit if he is still convicted of his sins at times?
    No. Conviction is proof that God is still giving him opportunity to repent.

17. Are there not other spirits in the world besides the Holy spirit?
    Yes.

18. How are we to know when the Holy Spirit is speaking to us?
    He will speak according to God's Word.

19. Does he always speak in an audible voice to us?
    No. He most frequently speaks through our conscience.

20. Of whom does he witness?
    "He shall testify of me," said Christ (John 15:26).

21. Name others besides those at Pentecost who received the baptism of the Holy Ghost in apostolic days.
    Cornelius (Acts 10); the Samaritans (Acts 8); Paul (Acts 9); twelve men of Ephesus (Acts 19).

22. To whom did Peter at Pentecost say the gift of the Holy Spirit is promised?

"Unto you [the Jews] and to your children, and to all that are afar off, even as many as the Lord our God shall call [all believers]" (Acts 2:39).

23. What is the purpose of the baptism of the Holy Spirit?
To give witnessing power (Acts 1:8).

24. How will all those who have the Holy Spirit feel toward all others who have him?
They will have fellowship with all who have him.

25. What are some of the fruits of those who have the Holy Spirit?
"Love, joy, peace, long-suffering, gentleness, goodness, faith, meekness, temperance" (Gal. 5:22, 23).

26. What are the gifts of the Spirit?
Special spiritual qualifications that he gives for God's service.

27. What are some of these gifts?
Wisdom; knowledge; faith; healing; miracles, etc. (I Cor. 12:9, 10).

28. Are they the same in all to whom they are given?
No. "There are diversities of operations" (I Cor. 12:6).

29. Of what value are these gifts?
To enable a person to edify and help God's people, to win souls for Christ, as well as build up himself in the faith.

30. Should they ever be manifested in a disorderly way?
No, "for God is not the author of confusion, but of peace, as in all churches of the saints" (I Cor. 14:33).

31. What great fruit of the Spirit must a man have in order to exercise the gifts of the Spirit properly?
Love (see I Cor. 13).

32. Is it possible to have a deception which we call a gift, but which is not a gift?
Yes, many are so deceived today.

33. How can we lose the gifts God has given us?
By losing our faith and failing to exercise them.

34. What is the most important spiritual gift?
Prophecy, or ministering God's Word (I Cor. 14:39).

35. How did the church at Corinth misuse the gifts of the Spirit?
   They used them to try to exalt themselves rather than to edify the church.

36. Should we seek these spiritual gifts?
   Yes, gifts may be sought, but love is of greater importance.

37. When are the gifts of the Spirit received?
   Either at the time of the Holy Spirit's baptism or afterward.

38. Does the Holy Spirit ever give instruction contrary to the will of God?
   No.

39. Does he ever teach contradictory to Christ's or the apostles' precepts?
   No.

40. How does he help us when we pray?
   He maketh intercession for us with groanings which cannot be uttered (Rom. 8:26).

Man, the Crown of Creation

1. Who made man?
   God.

2. Why did God make man?
   So that he could have a being in his own image who could love him.

3. When did God create man?
   On the sixth day of the creation week.

4. Of what did God form man's body?
   The dust of the earth.

5. In whose image did God make man?
   In God's image.

6. Where did the Lord place the first man that he made?
   In the Garden of Eden.

7. Was there anything else to him besides the body God gave him?

Yes, his soul, or spirit.

8. Was man sinful when he was made?
   No, he was pure and holy.

9. What was man to rule over?
   Over all the earth, including all the animals in the world.

10. What was the first thing that God told the man not to do?
    Not to eat of the tree of the knowledge of good and evil.

11. What was to become of the man if he should eat of it?
    He should die.

12. Of what substance did God form woman?
    Of one of Adam's ribs.

13. How did the man and woman compare with the angels?
    They were a little lower than the angels.

14. How did they compare with the other creatures of earth?
    They were more valuable in God's sight, were more intelligent and more wise.

15. Who is the greatest enemy of man?
    Satan.

16. How did he speak to Eve in Eden?
    Through the serpent.

17. What did the serpent succeed in getting Eve to do?
    Eat of the forbidden fruit.

18. Did Adam eat of it too?
    Yes.

19. What did God do with them after they had sinned?
    Drove them from Eden.

20. What tree did God keep them from eating the fruit of?
    The tree of life.

21. Did they die?
    Yes, they died spiritually at once and physically later.

22. Did their sin affect any others besides Adam and Eve?
    Yes, the whole human race.

23. Who was the first boy born into the world?
    Cain.
24. The second?
    Abel.
25. What was the first murder?
    Abel was slain by Cain.
26. What had been born into Cain's heart that had started him on the downward road?
    The seed of sin—a depraved, fallen nature.
27. Did the human race get better or worse after this?
    Worse.
28. What great judgment did God bring upon man in the time of Noah?
    He destroyed him with a flood.
29. After Noah's time what did the people try to do?
    All gather in one place, and build the tower of Babel.
30. Why did this displease God?
    He wanted the human race to populate the earth.
31. How did God scatter man over the earth at this time?
    By giving men different languages.
32. What race of mankind were God's chosen people?
    The Jews.
33. Did they always live true to God?
    No.
34. What man is called the "second Adam"?
    Christ.
35. Was any man ever born into the world without sin except Christ?
    No.
36. Did any man ever live without committing sin except Christ?
    No.
37. What is the allotted age of man's life?
    "Threescore years and ten"—seventy years.
38. Why does God let man live on the earth despite his wickedness?
    He wants to see man saved.

39. What becomes of the body of man at death?
    It returns to dust.
40. What becomes of man's soul at death?
    It lives forever in a future world.

Satan and Demons

1. What is the nature of Satan?
   He is a spirit.
2. Was he ever created, or did he exist always?
   He was probably created one time by God, before he
      became wicked.
3. Do we know where he came from to earth?
   Not certainly.
4. Where is his present abode?
   In hell.
5. What great sin did he cause to be committed that af-
      fected the whole human race?
   The sin of Adam and Eve in Eden.
6. Of what is he called "the father"?
   "Of lies" (John 8:44).
7. Whom was the greatest personage whom he tried to
      tempt?
   Christ.
8. Is Satan a personal being?
   Yes.
9. Does he have horns, a long tail, and carry a pitchfork?
   No, because he is a spirit.
10. Whom does he especially try to deceive?
    God's people.
11. Why does he not work so hard upon others?
    He already has them in his power.
12. Why is he called a murderer?
    Because he caused every murder that was ever com-
       mitted, from Cain's on down to now.
13. How much power does he have?
    More than human. He is mighty.

14. How then can we conquer him?
    We cannot, except by God's help.

15. By what other names is he known?
    The devil, meaning accuser, and Beelzebub, meaning
    the god of corruption.

16. Are there other bad spirits besides Satan, or Beelze-
    bub?
    Yes, there are demons.

17. How many demons are there?
    We do not know. Probably millions.

18. Are these demons almighty beings, like God?
    No, they are mighty, but they do not have all power.

19. Do they know all things as does God?
    No. They are limited in knowledge.

20. Do they have to stay in one place all the time?
    No. They have the power to move very rapidly.

21. How far can they go in tempting and harming people?
    No further than God permits them.

22. How does the devil tempt most people?
    By putting evil thoughts into their minds.

23. What is going to be the final punishment of Satan and
    the demons?
    They are to be punished in eternal fire forever.

24. How near to a person will Satan come if that person
    lets him?
    He will come in and take possession of him.

25. When Satan takes control of a man and lives in him,
    what has happened to him?
    He is possessed with demons.

26. How can a man who is possessed with demons get rid
    of them?
    By having Christian people pray that they be cast out.

27. Do Satan and his imps always appear just as they are?
    No, for they are great deceivers.

28. Whom do they particularly like to deceive?
    The children of God.

29. Who are called the children of Satan?
    Those who serve him in sin.

30. Why is Satan called the prince of this world?
    Because he and his imps now are having their way
    among the worldly people.
31. Why is he sometimes called the "god of this world"?
    Because most people follow him rather than follow
    God.
32. To what ravenous creature is he likened?
    To a roaring, hungry lion.
33. Is Satan bold as a lion?
    No, he flees when the righteous rebuke him.
34. How can a person overcome Satan?
    By prayer, and work in God's service.
35. If a person is once delivered from Satan, can Satan
    cause him to fall?
    Yes, if that person yields to temptation.
36. How can we defend ourselves against Satan?
    By keeping close to God.
37. Will Satan ever quit tempting us, so long as we live?
    No.
38. Do the heathens believe in a devil?
    Yes, and some of them worship him.
39. Does he help the heathen when they pray to him?
    No, he works against them.
40. How can we help the heathen to overcome Satan and
    his imps?
    By taking Christ, who is the victor over all demons, to
    them.

Angels

1. What does the word "angel" mean?
   Messenger.
2. Are there different kinds of angels?
   Yes, good and bad.
3. What is the nature of an angel?
   It is a spirit.

4. Do they ever appear in human form?
   Yes.
5. Did angels always exist?
   No. They were created by God.
6. Are they the spirits of dead people?
   No. They are a higher order of beings. They never were people.
7. Are they persons?
   Yes. Just as much so as men are.
8. Can we always see them?
   No. Sometimes they are around us and are hidden from our view.
9. Do they have wings?
   No. They often looked like men when they appeared.
10. What is the work of good angels?
    To minister to God's people.
11. Are they a higher order of creating than men?
    Yes.
12. In what way are they higher?
    They were created immortal.
13. What was it that God made for man that the angels desired to look into?
    The plan of salvation.
14. Did all the angels God created stay good?
    No, some of them sinned.
15. Where are those angels that sinned?
    Bound in chains, awaiting the day of judgment.
16. What man spoken of in Luke died, and was carried by the angels to paradise?
    Lazarus (See Luke 16).
17. To whom did angels announce the coming of Christ?
    To Mary, and to the shepherds of Bethlehem.
18. Name some places in Christ's life where angels appeared to him.
    After the temptation; in Gethsemane; at the cross; at the resurrection, and at the ascension.
19. When will angels appear with Christ again?
    At his second coming.

20. Do angels have all power, as God does?
    No, they are limited by God.
21. How do they help God's people?
    Usually by strengthening them in temptation, and
    guarding them from danger.
22. What will be the final punishment of the angels who
    sinned?
    They will receive the same punishment as will the dem-
    ons.
23. What men in the New Testament do we read of who
    saw angels in visions?
    Joseph, Peter, Cornelius, Paul, and John.
24. In Old Testament times what did they think would hap-
    pen to a person who saw an angel?
    They thought he would die at once.
25. Do we always know when angels help us?
    No. Sometimes they come to our rescue and we never
    realize it.
26. Name some of the angels who have appeared at var-
    ious times.
    Gabriel, Michael.
27. Who will announce the final judgment scene?
    An angel.
28. At what important place did God station an angel back
    in Eden?
    At the entrance to guard the way of the tree of life.
29. What causes great joy among the angels of heaven?
    The salvation of sinners.
30. How many angels are there?
    Multitudes. More than can be numbered by us.
31. What will be their work at the end of the world?
    To separate the good people from the bad.
32. Is it possible for us to know all about angels now?
    No. We will find that out in heaven.
33. Who gave us to understand that the angels never mar-
    ry, as do human beings?
    Jesus.

34. Do the angels ever die?
No. They live forever.

35. Are there some things the angels do not know?
Yes. They do not know when Christ will come again, and many other things, possibly.

36. Whom do the guardian angels especially help?
Children.

37. How do the angels occupy themselves in heaven?
In a chorus of joy—praising God.

38. When did Jesus say he could summon the angels to help him if he wanted to?
In Gethsemane.

39. Who in Christ's time did not believe in angels?
The sect of the Sadducees.

The Church

1. What is the meaning of the word "church"?
Congregation or assembly of called-out ones.

2. Who built the New Testament church?
Christ (See Matt. 16:18).

3. Who make up Christ's church?
All his people in heaven and on earth (Eph. 3:15).

4. What is a local congregation of the church made up of?
God's people meeting in a certain locality regularly, for worship.

5. How many times is the word church used in the New Testament of the local congregations?
Ninety-two.

6. Name three local congregations of the early church.
Jerusalem (Acts 8:1), Corinth (I Cor. 1:2), Philadelphia (Rev. 3:7).

7. Of what should the local congregation be representative?
Of the general church, or church universal.

8. Does God recognize sinners as members of a local church?
   No.

9. Name some New Testament examples of local congregations that were rejected by Christ.
   Ephesus (Rev. 1:5), Pergamos (vs. 16) and Sardis (ch. 3:3).

10. When does Christ cease to acknowledge a local congregation?
    When it has so forsaken the faith that it no longer represents his universal church.

11. Why is the church called Christ's body?
    Because he uses it in this world—as we use our physical bodies—to express himself.

12. Who is the chief cornerstone of the church?
    Christ.

13. Who else with Christ constitutes the foundation?
    The apostles and prophets.

14. What figure is used in the New Testament to show the near relationship of the church to Christ?
    She is called his bride.

15. How did Christ purchase this bride for himself?
    With his own blood, on Calvary's cross (Eph. 5:25).

16. Who is the head of the church?
    Christ (Eph. 1:22).

17. Who adds the members to God's church?
    The Lord (Acts 2:47).

18. How much of a unit should God's people be?
    As much as the Father and Son (John 17:21).

19. Who feeds this church?
    God's ministers (Acts 20:28).

20. What do they feed the church?
    The word of God.

21. Who is it that persecutes the church?
    The wicked, some of whom are religious.

22. Why did Jesus build his church?
    So that it might go on with his work in the world.

23. What is the work of the church?
  To preach the gospel to all nations.
24. When was it built, and set in operation for this work?
  On the Day of Pentecost.
25. Who is the organizer of the church?
  God.
26. Who puts the church members in their proper places?
  The Holy Spirit.
27. Whom should we recognize as members?
  All whom God recognizes and adds—those who have been born again.
28. Does a formal joining of a denomination make a person a member of the universal church of Christ?
  No. "Ye must be born again" (John 3:7).
29. What does the world expect of a person who is a church member?
  That his life be consistent with his profession.
30. Are there any hypocrites in God's church?
  No, although they may profess and be recognized as members for a time.
31. Who are the officers of God's church?
  Ministers—including pastors, teachers, gospel workers, and deacons, or helpers.
32. What great false church took the place of God's true church in the world for over a thousand years?
  The Roman Catholic Church.
33. Who led the Reformation movement of the sixteenth century against Rome?
  Martin Luther.
34. What great man was instrumental in bringing about a reformation movement in England?
  John Wesley.
35. What is the work of a pastor of the church?
  To care for and preach to a local congregation.
36. What is the work of an evangelist?
  To preach the gospel in new fields, or help put enthusiasm into the older congregations.
37. The deacon?

To assist the pastor and church, either financially or in spiritual things.
38. How should the members feel toward one another?
    There should be complete fellowship.
39. What is the final home of the church?
    Heaven.
40. When will all of us who are saved be admitted to that home?
    At the day of judgment.

Salvation

1. What do we mean by salvation?
   To be saved from sin and its penalty, and to be received by God.
2. Who is the author of our salvation?
   God.
3. Whom is he willing to save?
   All who come to him.
4. Who died that we might be saved?
   Christ.
5. What do we call Christ's death for us?
   The atonement.
6. When was the atonement first mentioned to man?
   In the Garden of Eden (see Gen. 3:15).
7. Before Christ came, who were God's chosen people?
   The Jews.
8. After he came, whom did he say he wanted to come and get saved?
   The whole world.
9. What does salvation do for us?
   It makes us new creatures.
10. Can we get it by any work that we do?
    No, it is a gift from God.
11. What verse in the Bible telling us about salvation is often called "the golden gospel"?
    John 3:16.

12. What must take place before we can be saved?
    We must be convicted of sin, and spiritually awakened.

13. What next must we do?
    Repent, or turn from our sins.

14. If we have taken anything from anyone, what must we do with it?
    Return it, or if that is impossible make it right with him some other way.

15. If we have injured anyone what must we do?
    Ask that person's forgiveness.

16. What then must we have before we can be saved?
    Faith in God.

17. What does salvation do for us?
    It makes us right with God.

18. What does it deliver us from?
    Sin.

19. Will it take away our sinful habits?
    Yes.

20. Who was our Master before we were saved?
    Satan.

21. Who is afterward?
    Christ.

22. Must we be baptized before we get saved?
    No. We must repent and believe first.

23. Do we always shout, or cry, or make some demonstration when we are saved?
    Not necessarily.

24. When is the time to get saved?
    In our youth.

25. At what age do most people get saved?
    Between fifteen and twenty-one.

26. Why is it more difficult for an older person to get salvation?
    He is hardened in his sins.

27. What are we saved for?
    To work for God.

28. How old should a child be before he can get saved?
    Old enough to realize he is a sinner and know how to
    get saved.

29. Who convicts the sinner of his sin?
    The Holy Spirit.

30. What two things are accomplished in our salvation?
    We are forgiven, and we are made new creatures.

31. Can we sin after we are saved?
    Yes, but we do not need to do so.

32. Why is salvation called a tower?
    It keeps us safe from Satan's darts.

33. Why is it called a lamp?
    It lights our way and thus guides our feet heavenward.

34. How long will salvation keep us?
    Forever.

35. If we sin, what happens?
    We incur the displeasure of God.

36. What kingdom do we leave when we get saved?
    The devil's kingdom of darkness.

37. Whose kingdom do we get into?
    Jesus'—a kingdom of light.

38. What are some of the good fruits of salvation?
    Love, joy, peace, hope, faith.

39. Will salvation keep us from making mistakes?
    No. We are still human.

40. Will it keep us from committing intentional, willful
    sins?
    Yes.

Christian Conduct

1. What is the greatest commandment?
   To love the Lord with all our heart, soul, mind, and
   strength.

2. What is the next greatest commandment?
   To love our neighbor as ourself.

3. Should we love just our friends?
   No. We should also love our enemies.
4. What is faith?
   Faith is the assurance that is fixed in confidence in God and his Word.
5. Can we please God without faith?
   No.
6. What great chapter of the Bible tells us about faith?
   Hebrews 11.
7. Whom should we obey?
   God, parents, rulers.
8. When should we not obey men?
   When they try to make us work against God.
9. What else should we obey?
   God's Word.
10. What is prayer?
    Talking to God.
11. Why is it necessary?
    To praise God, and let him know our needs.
12. Whom should we pray for?
    Everybody, particularly those in need.
13. Whom else do we neglect when we neglect the poor?
    Christ.
14. What should we do with the poor?
    Help them all we can.
15. Who became poor to help us become rich?
    Christ.
16. Where does the Christian find happiness?
    In living for God.
17. It it possible to be always happy and live away from God?
    No.
18. Will money, or fine clothes bring lasting happiness?
    No.
19. Who are tempted?
    All of God's people.
20. What should we do when tempted to sin?
    Pray and rebuke the devil.

21. Is temptation sin?
    No. Just yielding to it is sin.

22. How can we help the sick?
    Visit and pray for them.

23. Where does sickness come from?
    Sometimes from Satan, sometimes from natural causes, and sometimes from God.

24. When we pray for the sick what should we expect God to do for them?
    Heal them.

25. What is persecution?
    Bad treatment of the Christian people by people of the world who are against Him.

26. How should we act toward those who persecute us?
    Pray for them.

27. How much should a husband love his wife?
    As Christ loved the church (see Eph. 5:25).

28. How should a wife regard her husband?
    Be submissive to him, as to the Lord.

29. How should children behave toward parents?
    Obey them in the Lord.

30. What should parents do to keep the respect of the children?
    Set them a good example and not provoke them to evil.

31. How should a workman act toward his employer?
    Conscientiously—he should do his best.

32. How must an employer act toward the man who works for him?
    He should treat him as a brother, kindly and considerately.

33. Should a Christian indulge in worldly amusement?
    No.

34. What are worldly amusements?
    Any that keep one from being spiritual.

35. Who can work for God?
    All who are saved.

36. What can they do for God?
    Whatever their natural qualifications and God's gifts qualify them to do.
37. After we are saved, who owns us and our possessions?
    God.
38. What does he want us to do with a part of our possessions?
    Give it to the work of his kingdom.
39. What should be the Christian's attitude toward the government?
    He should support it and pray for the rulers.
40. How should he regard the law of the land?
    He should obey it.

Last Things

1. How do we know all men must die?
    The Bible says, "It is appointed unto men once to die" (Heb. 9:27).
2. What is death?
    The separation of the soul from the body.
3. What becomes of the body after death?
    It returns to the earth—becomes dust again.
4. Should death be a terror to men?
    No. It is not a terror for the righteous.
5. What other kind of death is there besides physical death?
    Spiritual death.
6. How long does the soul live in eternity?
    Forever.
7. When will man receive an immortal body?
    At the resurrection.
8. Who has already received his full immortality?
    Christ.
9. Will our earthly body that went to dust ever be used again by the soul?
    Yes. It will be changed into our immortal body.

10. What heavenly beings are already immortal?
    The angels.
11. Where do the souls of the righteous go at death?
    To paradise.
12. What kind of place is paradise?
    A place of happiness and joy.
13. Where do the souls of the wicked go at death?
    To a place of punishment.
14. Why are they held in this place of punishment?
    Because of their sins.
15. How long will the righteous and wicked remain in
    these places?
    Until the day of judgment.
16. When will Christ return to judge the earth?
    No one knows when he will come but God.
17. Whom will he bring with him when he comes?
    The angels, and souls of the departed.
18. Where will he appear?
    In the clouds of heaven.
19. What will the righteous do when He comes?
    Praise Him and rejoice.
20. What will the wicked do?
    Try to hide from Him.
21. What sect of the Jews in Christ's time said there would
    be no resurrection?
    The Sadducees.
22. Whose resurrection is a proof that some day we shall
    be resurrected?
    Christ's.
23. Who of the human race will be resurrected from their
    graves?
    All who have died.
24. What great chapter in the New Testament is chiefly
    about the resurrection?
    I Corinthians 15.
25. What else is the day of judgment called?
    The last great day.

26. Who will be the judge?
    Christ.

27. Into what two great classes will Christ divide the world at the final judgment?
    Good and bad.

28. For what will Christ judge all?
    For the deeds they have done in their bodies.

29. What will finally become of the earth?
    It will be burned up.

30. Why will the earth be destroyed?
    It will no longer be needed for man's dwelling place.

31. How were the people of the earth once destroyed?
    With a universal flood.

32. Why will the destruction be by fire instead of by water the next time?
    Because God has so decreed.

33. Where will the righteous spend eternity?
    In heaven.

34. Can we understand now all that heaven will be like?
    No. It is impossible for us to understand it all.

35. What kind of place will it be?
    A place of the greatest possible happiness.

36. Will we know our loved ones in heaven?
    Yes.

37. Where will the wicked spend eternity.
    In hell.

38. What kind of a place is hell?
    A place of everlasting fire.

39. What is there between heaven and hell?
    A great gulf.

40. How long will both heaven and hell last?
    Forever.

HISTORY OF THE CHURCH

The trials and triumphs of the church through the ages are a source of inspiration to all Christians. Early church history is revealed to us in Scripture, and later church history is necessary to a knowledge of Bible prophecy and fulfillment. Hence, a drill on this subject is essential to an understanding of Scripture.

1. What is the first period of church history called, and what is its date?

   The Apostolic Church. From the ascension of Christ, A.D. 30, to the death of the apostle John, about A.D. 100.

2. With what great event was the church started on its mission?

   The coming of the Holy Ghost at Pentecost.

3. What were the two great city centers of early Christianity?

   Jerusalem and Antioch.

4. In the early part of this period by what people was the gospel accepted?

   The Jews.

5. What great campaigns were launched from Antioch that led to the rapid spread of the church among the Gentiles?

Paul's missionary journeys.

6. Under whose reign did the first persecution against Christians start?

The Emperor Nero's.

7. What was the spiritual state of the church at the end of the first century?

It is called the "age of shadows," for the Book of Revelation indicates that the tone of spiritual life was decreasing.

8. What was the second period of church history?

The Persecuted Church. From the death of the apostle John, A.D. 100, to the Edict of Constantine, A.D. 313.

9. How many organized persecutions under Roman Emperors were directed against the church in this and the former period?

Ten.

10. Why did the heathen emperors regard the church as unpatriotic?

It refused to sanction emperor worship.

11. What great learned Stoic emperor persecuted Christianity under this period?

Marcus Aurelius.

12. Name three martyrs who gave their lives for Christ at this time.

Ignatius, Polycarp, and Justin Martyr.

13. What change in church organization arose during this period?

Originally bishops and elders were synonymous terms, applied to the same officer. Now, bishops came to denote a higher order than the elders and deacons.

14. Name four famous church fathers, or writers of theology during this period.

Clement of Alexandria, Origen, Tertullian, and Cyprian.

15. What was the third period of church history?
    The Imperial Church. From the Edict of Constantine,
    A.D. 313, to the fall of Rome, A.D. 476.

16. What was the Edict of Constantine?
    Constantine, the first Christian Roman Emperor, is-
    sued an Edict of Toleration in 313 which officially
    ended the persecution of Christians by the empire.

17. What did the binding together of church and state pro-
    duce that was not good?
    Paganism entered the church in its government and
    practice.

18. What great church council was held in A.D. 325?
    The Council of Nicea.

19. Who were some great leaders of this period?
    Athanasius, Ambrose of Milan, John Chrysostom,
    Jerome, and Augustine.

20. What five great sees of the church arose at this time?
    Rome, Constantinople, Antioch, Jerusalem, and Alex-
    andria.

21. What two eventually became rivals for supremacy?
    Rome and Constantinople.

22. What was the fourth period of church history?
    The Medieval Church, from the fall of Rome, in 476,
    to the fall of Constantinople, in 1453.

23. When were the popes recognized as universal bishops?
    In 445, Leo the Great was thus recognized by Valen-
    tian III, emperor of the West, and in 606, Phocas,
    emperor of the East, thus recognized Gregory the
    Great.

24. What pope is thought of as reaching the height of
    papal authority?
    Hildebrand, or Gregory VII (1085).

25. What great false religion arose in the seventh century
    that tried to destroy the Christian church?
    Mohammedanism.

26. When did the Greek Church separate from the Western
    or Latin church?
    In A.D. 1054.

27. What great movement of the Middle Ages was begun by the church in the latter part of the twelfth century?
The Crusades against the Saracens.

28. What great pre-Reformation reformers arose during this period?
John Wycliffe, John Huss, and Savonarola.

29. What is the fifth period of church history?
The Reformation. From the fall of Constantinople in 1453 to the Thirty Years' War in 1648.

30. What great invention in 1455 helped usher in the rapid spread of the Reformation?
Printing from moveable type, by Gutenberg.

31. Who was the leader of the Sixteenth Century Reformation?
Martin Luther.

32. What countries were especially prominent in the Reformation cause?
Germany, Switzerland, Scandinavia, France, the Netherlands, England, and Scotland.

33. What was the counter-reformation?
A reformation within the Roman Catholic Church to oppose Protestantism.

34. Who were the Protestant leaders of this period?
Luther, Calvin, and Knox.

35. What was the sixth period of church history?
The Modern Period. From the Thirty Years' War, in 1648, to the present time.

36. What great English leader brought about a distinct revival in the eighteenth century?
John Wesley.

37. Who is regarded as the founder of modern missions?
William Carey, of England.

38. Name some other great leaders of the modern period.
Charles Wesley, George Whitefield, Jonathan Edwards.

39. What great movement is characterizing present-day Christianity?
That toward a united church.

40. About how many large Protestant denominations are in existance in the United States today?

Two hundred and twelve, according to a late census.

CHAPTERS AND VERSES TO LOOK UP

Although all the verses and chapters in the Bible are good, there are some outstanding portions of Scripture with which we should be familiar.

This section is good for verse-finding contests. Match one side against another, and see who finds the most verses and chapters the quickest, or out of a group see who can get the best record for quick verse- and chapter-finding. Too, the leader could quote the verse or part of the chapter and ask the class where it is found.

Verses

1. In the beginning God created the heaven and the earth. —Gen. 1:1.
2. And I will put enmity between thee and the woman, and between thy seed and her seed; it shall bruise thy head, and thou shalt bruise his heel.—Gen. 3:15.
3. And I will make of thee a great nation, and I will bless thee, and make thy name great; and thou shalt be a blessing.—Gen. 12:2.

4. And when the Lord saw that he turned aside to see, God called unto him out of the midst of the bush, and said, Moses, Moses. And he said, Here am I.—Exod. 3:4.

5. Thou shalt have no other gods before me.—Exod. 20:3.

6. Honor thy father and thy mother: that thy days may be long upon the land which the Lord thy God giveth thee.—Exod. 20:12.

7. So Moses the servant of the Lord died there in the land of Moab, according to the word of the Lord. —Deut. 34:5.

8. And Elijah came unto all the people, and said, How long halt ye between two opinions? If the Lord be God, follow him: but if Baal, then follow him. And the people answered him not a word.—I Kings 18:21.

9. And when all the people saw it, they fell on their faces: and they said, The Lord, he is the God; the Lord, he is the God. —I Kings 18:39.

10. But there was none like unto Ahab, which did sell himself to work wickedness in the sight of the Lord, whom Jezebel his wife stirred up.—I Kings 21:25.

11. And he did evil in the sight of the Lord, and walked in the way of his father, and in the way of his mother, and in the way of Jeroboam the son of Nebat, who made Israel to sin.—I Kings 22:52.

12. Then said his wife unto him, Dost thou still retain thine integrity? curse God, and die.—Job. 2:9.

13. Blessed is the man that walketh not in the counsel of the ungodly, nor standeth in the way of sinners, nor sitteth in the seat of the scornful.—Ps. 1:1.

14. The Lord is my shepherd: I shall not want.—Ps. 23:1.

15. O fear the Yord, ye his saints: for there is no want to them that fear him.—Ps. 34:9.

16. The fear of the Lord is the beginning of wisdom: a good understanding have all they that do his commandments: his praise endureth for ever.—Ps. 111:10.

17. Thy word is a lamp unto my feet, and light unto my path.—Ps. 119:105.

18. Praise ye the Lord. Praise the Lord, O my soul.—Ps. 146:1.

19. For unto us a child is born, unto us a son is given: the government shall be upon his shoulder: and his name shall be called Wonderful, Counselor, The mighty God, The everlasting Father, The Prince of Peace.—Isa. 9:6.

20. Then answered Amos, and said to Amaziah, I was no prophet, neither was I a prophet's son; but I was an herdman, and a gatherer of sycamore fruit.—Amos 7:14.

21. And she shall bring forth a son, and thou shalt call his name Jesus: for he shall save his people from their sins.—Matt. 1:21.

22. Jesus said unto him, Thou shalt love the Lord thy God with all thy heart, and with all thy soul, and with all thy mind.—Matt. 22:37.

23. And he said unto them, Go ye into all the world, and preach the gospel to every creature.—Mark 16:15.

24. So then after the Lord had spoken unto them, he was received up into heaven, and sat on the right hand of God.—Mark 16:19.

25. Glory to God in the highest, and on earth peace, good will toward men.—Luke 2:14.

26. But Jesus called them unto him, and said, Suffer the little children to come unto me, and forbid them not: for such is the kingdom of God.—Luke 18:16.

27. For God so loved the world, that he gave his only begotten Son, that whosoever believeth in him should not perish, but have everlasting life.—John 3:16.

28. Jesus wept.—John 11:35.

29. Neither is there salvation in any other: for there is none other name under heaven given among men, whereby we must be saved.—Acts 4:12.

30. And he trembling and astonished said, Lord, what wilt thou have me do? And the Lord said unto him, Arise and go into the city, and it shall be told thee what thou must do.—Acts 9:6.

31. For I am not ashamed of the gospel of Christ: for it is the power of God unto salvation to every one that believeth; to the Jew first, and also to the Greek.—Rom. 1:16.

32. Love worketh no ill to his neighbor: therefore love is the fulfilling of the law.—Rom. 13:10.

33. Therefore let no man glory in men. For all things are yours.—I Cor. 3:21.

34. Let the word of Christ dwell in you richly in all wisdom; teaching and admonishing one another in psalms and hymns and spiritual songs, singing with grace in your heart to the Lord.—Cor. 3:16.

35. And whatsoever ye do in word or deed, do all in the name of the Lord Jesus, giving thanks to God and the Father by him.—Col. 3:17.

36. Now unto the King eternal, immortal, invisible, the only wise God, be honor and glory for ever and ever. Amen.— I Tim. 1:17.

37. All scripture is given by inspiration of God, and is profitable for doctrine, for reproof, for correction, for instruction in righteousness.—II Tim. 3:16.

38. Choosing rather to suffer affliction with the people of God, than to enjoy the pleasures of sin for a season. —Heb. 11:25.

39. He that loveth not knoweth not God; for God is love. —I John 4:8.

40. The grace of our Lord Jesus-Christ be with you all. Amen.—Rev. 22:21.

Great Chapters

1. Creation chapter. Genesis 1.
2. Law chapter. Exodus 20.
3. Tree and chaff. Psalm 1.
4. Shepherd Psalm. Psalm 23.
5. Shortest Psalm. Psalm 117.
6. Bible Lover's Psalm. Psalm 119.

7. Hallelujah Psalms. Psalms 146-150.
8. The Suffering Messiah. Isaiah 53.
9. The Gospel in Isaiah. Isaiah 55.
10. Sermon on the Mount. Matthew 5, 6, 7.
11. The Christmas Story. Luke 2.
12. The Divine Word. John 1.
13. The New Birth Chapter. John 3.
14. Comfort Chapter. John 14.
15. Love Chapter. I Corinthians 13.
16. Chapter on Last Days. II Timothy 3.
17. Our Life in Christ. Colossians 3.
18. The New-creation Chapter. Revelations 22.

MEMORY WORK

This memory course is particularly adapted to the junior child, although much of it may be learned by primaries, and all by those above the junior grade. Material for a three-year course is herewith provided.

First Year

GOD'S WORKS

1. Creation of the world. Gen. 1:1-5.
2. Creation of man. Gen. 1:26-28, 31.
3. God of earth and heaven. Ps. 24:1-4.
4. The King of Glory. Ps. 24:7-10.
5. His glorious heavens. Ps. 19:1-6.

TEACHINGS OF JESUS

1. The Beatitudes. Matt. 5:3-12.
2. The gracious invitation. Matt. 11:28-30.
3. Elements of discipleship. Mark 8:34-37.
4. How to attain to greatness. Mark 10:43-45.
5. The great commandments. Mark 12:30, 31.
6. The golden gospel. John 3:14-16.

7. Mansions in Father's house. John 14:1-3.
8. Concerning the children. Mark 10:14-16.
9. The Good Shepherd. John 10:11-16.
10. The Golden Rule. Matt. 7:12.

FAMOUS PSALMS

(Note: These may be used as supplementary work.)

1. The Safe Refuge. Psalm 91.
2. A Song of Joy. Psalm 96.
3. A Psalm of Praise. Psalm 100.
4. God, the Preserver. Psalm 121.

Second Year

GOD'S TEACHINGS

1. Concerning his law. Ps. 19:7-10.
2. Worship him only. Exod. 20:1-6.
3. Our relation to God. Exod. 20:7-11.
4. Our relation to others. Exod. 20:12-17.
5. God's blessed man. Ps. 1:1-3.
6. The wicked man. Ps. 1:4-6.
7. Reward of keeping his commandments. Prov. 3:1-6.
8. Think of God everywhere. Deut. 6:4-7.
9. When to remember God. Eccles. 12:1-4, 13, 14.
10. How to succeed. Josh. 1:8-9.

PLAN OF SALVATION

1. God's invitation to us. Isa. 55:1-3.
2. How to seek him. Isa. 55:6-8.
3. Contained in his Word. Isa. 55:9-11.
4. Christ's atonement for us. Isa. 53:3-7.
5. Prophecy of the Christ child. Isa. 9:6, 7.
6. The Magnificat. Luke 1:46-55.
7. The angels' song. Luke 2:8-11.
8. The Manger Babe. Luke 2:12-14.
9. The Word that lived among men. John 1:1-4.
10. The new birth. John 3:3, 5-8.

CHRIST'S DEATH TO HIS ASCENSION

1. The Seven Words from the Cross. Luke 23:34, 43; John 19:26, 27; Mark 15:34; John 19:28, 30; Luke 23:46.
2. The resurrection. Matt 28:1-4.
3. Others to hear the good news. Matt. 28:5-7.
4. The world to hear it. Matt. 28:16, 18-20.
5. The ascension. Acts 1:7-9.

Third Year

WORSHIPING GOD

1. Acknowledging his gift. Ps. 103:1-5.
2. His great goodness. Ps. 103:10-14.
3. Our shepherd. Psalm 23.
4. A prayer of penitence. Ps. 19:12-14.
5. A humble prayer. Ps. 139:1-4, 23, 24.
6. The house of prayer. Ps. 84:1-3.
7. God's precious presence. Ps. 84:9-12.
8. The Lord's Prayer. Matt. 6:9-13.
9. Jesus' great prayer. John 17:1-10.
10. A prayer of benediction. Jude 24, 25.

CHRISTIAN CHARACTER BUILDING

1. Depends upon the Holy Spirit. Acts 2:1-4.
2. We must be consecrated to God. Rom. 12:1, 2.
3. Our bodies are God's temples. I Cor. 3:16, 17.
4. The greatest thing in the world. I Cor. 13:1-3.
5. What love does. I Cor. 13:4-8, 13.
6. The goal we strive for. Phil. 3:13-14.
7. What to think upon. Phil. 4:8.
8. The Christian graces. II Pet. 1:5-7.
9. The Christian's armor. Eph. 6:10-18.
10. Doers as well as hearers. Jas. 1:22-27.

THE HEAVENLY HOME

1. The new earth. Rev. 22:1-4.
2. All invited to that abode. Rev. 22:14, 17.

QUESTIONS FOR PRIMARIES

These questions are suited to children just starting to school, up to nine years of age.

Old Testament

1. Who made the grass and trees and flowers?
   God.
2. Who was the first man?
   Adam.
3. What man once built a big boat when God sent a big rain?
   Noah.
4. Who led the children of Israel across the Red Sea?
   Moses.
5. What shepherd boy killed a giant?
   David.
6. Who was taken to heaven in a chariot of fire?
   Elijah.
7. Who saw in a dream a ladder reaching to heaven?
   Jacob.
8. Who had a coat of many colors?
   Joseph.

9. Who prayed that the Lord would give her a little boy?
   Hannah.
10. Who was cast into a den of lions?
    Daniel.
11. Whom did God once call three times in the night?
    Samuel.
12. What prophet did the ravens feed at a brook?
    Elijah.
13. What strong man killed a lion with his hands?
    Sampson.
14. What did the spies carry from the land of Canaan?
    A bunch of grapes.
15. Who buried Moses?
    God.
16. Why did the people build the tower of Babel?
    To try to reach heaven.
17. What three boys did a bad king throw into a fiery furnace?
    Shadrach, Meshach, and Abednego.
18. What birds did the children of Israel eat in the desert?
    Quails.
19. What big house did the Israelites worship in?
    The Temple.
20. What man was swallowed by a big fish.
    Jonah.

New Testament

1. Who was born in a stable in Bethlehem?
   Jesus.
2. How old was Jesus when he talked with the doctors in the temple?
   Twelve years old.
3. What man baptized a great many people and was called the Baptist?
   John the Baptist.

4. How long did Jesus once go without eating?
   Forty days and forty nights.

5. What man climbed up into a tree to see Jesus?
   Zacchaeus.

6. Where did Jesus talk to a woman at a well?
   In Samaria.

7. What did Jesus do for a poor widow's son?
   Raised him from the dead.

8. How many people did Jesus feed at one time with five
   loaves of bread and two fishes?
   Five thousand.

9. What did Jesus once do for little children?
   He blessed them.

10. Whom did Jesus die for?
    All of us.

11. What man made three missionary journeys?
    Paul.

12. What did some heathen people at Lystra do to Paul?
    Stoned him.

13. What young man of Lystra preached with Paul?
    Timothy.

14. What did Paul and Silas do when the wicked people of
    Philippi put them in jail?
    They sang hymns and prayed.

15. In what big city did a mob try to kill Paul?
    Jerusalem.

16. Where did Paul go to be tried before the king?
    To Rome.

17. What happened on the way?
    Paul's ship was sunk.

18. How did the people get to the shore?
    They swam.

19. Who wrote about Jesus' life?
    Matthew, Mark, Luke, and John.

20. Who wrote the last book in the Bible?
    The apostle John.

SPECIAL QUESTIONS FOR JUNIORS

These questions are for children nine to twelve years of age. They may be used in social meetings of the class for a sort of Bible game, or as supplementary questions to class-work.

1. What is the Word of God?
   The Bible.
2. Who wrote the Bible?
   Prophets and apostles.
3. If man wrote it, how is it the Word of God?
   The Holy Spirit inspired them.
4. What does it mean to be inspired by the Holy Spirit?
   He helped them to know what to write and how to write it.
5. Why is it wrong to take God's name in vain by swearing?
   Because his name is sacred and holy.
6. What does it mean to lie?
   To tell something that you know is not so.
7. Why is it wrong to lie?
   Because neither God nor people like one who does it.
8. Who said not to steal?
   God.

9. What places in the land are kept for people who take
   things that do not belong to them?
   Jails, penitentiaries, and reform schools.

10. Name some things that tobacco does for growing boys
    who use it.
    It stunts their growth, makes their minds dull; and
    keeps them from serving God as he wants them to.

11. Why should we respect the Lord's Day?
    Because the Lord wants us to give a day to him.

12. How can we honor our parents.
    By obeying them and following their advice.

13. What is promised us for obeying our parents?
    A long life.

14. What should we think about?
    Only things that are pure.

15. What will cause impure thoughts?
    Bad books, bad pictures, and filthy stories.

16. Who is God?
    A spirit, uncreated and perfect.

17. Are there more Gods than one?
    No.

18. What three persons make up this one God?
    The Father, Son (Jesus), and Holy Spirit.

19. Of what did God create all things?
    Of nothing that we know of (Heb. 11:3).

20. What are angels?
    Created spirits.

21. Who is the chief of the evil angels?
    Beelzebub.

22. Of what two parts does a man consist?
    Body and soul.

23. Of what did God create man's body?
    Dust.

24. What is sin?
    Disobedience to God's laws.

25. Can we get out of sin ourselves?
    No. God must help us.

26. Whom did God give us to lift us out of sin?
    Jesus.
27. What two natures had Christ?
    He was both human and divine.
28. Who helps us to believe in Christ?
    His Holy Spirit.
29. What happens if we do not obey the Spirit?
    We grow hardened in sin.
30. What is justification?
    A setting aside of the punishment for sin.
31. How do we get saved?
    By praying, and believing in the Lord, forsaking our
      sins, and living for Christ.
32. Can God's church ever be destroyed?
    No. (See Matt. 16:18).
33. How can one keep saved?
    By praying, working for God, and reading one's Bible.
34. Who will judge the world at the last day?
    Jesus. (Matt. 25:31-33).
35. What will become of the righteous after the judgment?
    They will enter heaven.
36. What will become of the wicked after the judgment?
    They will be turned into hell.
37. What is prayer?
    Talking to God.
38. Whom should we pray for?
    Everybody.
39. Why should we be baptized?
    Because Jesus told his ministers to baptize all believers
      (Matt. 28:19).
40. Whom should we make our lives pattern after?
    Jesus.